# Of Broken Things

## A Collection of Poems and Ponderings

By, Laura West Hall

# Of Broken Things

A Collection of Poems and Ponderings

Printed by Amazon Kindle Direct Publishing

First printing, 2022.

Follow Laura West Hall on Facebook, Instagram, and @LauraHallparty on Twitter.

ISBN: 9798809824606

Cover image by Abigail Hall

# TABLE OF CONTENTS

# PREFACE

***OF BROKEN THINGS*** *starts in a dark place. It's the place in the middle of chaos, when we can't find ourselves, let alone see the best in others or the world. When I started this book, I was in a deep hole, as you will see reflected in the themes of some of the poems. My health was plummeting, just as the pandemic started, and the political unrest around the U.S. and the world was ramping up. It's been a few heavy years, hasn't it? You will definitely feel that collective frustration at times when you read this book. Still, it's a place we need to go together.*

*In many ways, this book was a form of therapy for me. Writing was a place to find myself again at the end of a long tough career that left me feeling spent and broken.  If you look around you, or within, and see brokenness, take this journey with me. I promise it gets better. Don't give up. Take a break when you need to, and just breathe. Whether you have emerged from the fog, or are still in it, please keep reading. You will feel lighter in the end.*

*It's like cleaning out a junk drawer. You may find some useful tools, some things you can get rid of, and maybe a few gems you didn't even know were lurking there, right under your nose.*

# LOSING TIME

## RUNNING OUT OF TEETH

The zipper is closing.
And I'm running out of teeth.
Dust covers everything and everything is covered.

I punch my fist into the sun,
Pull out the juice, the ideas, the portraits of meaning
that beat at me to be released.

The leaves are all purple and orange now.
Beautiful and terrifying.
More teeth.

I kick the hour glasses, waiting for a stir.
The gears turn as I waste the minutes. What's the rush? Why now?
Why at all?
More teeth.

Just do it, I say. Just be it.

I splatter some paint on the canvas. My fingers, in a panic,
smear and try to make sense.
More color? More texture?
I cut and rip it to shreds.
I type faster. I weave stronger. I sing higher. I prose longer.

How can I remove it all in time, before this lifetime
of inspiration and fire is extinguished?
How can I jump start myself into productivity,
when daydreaming my creations satiates?

More teeth.
Only I can give this. Only you can give that.
Give it now. The zipper is closing.

**FLATLINING**

Old man, Democracy,
held up by a cane of fragile ideals.
He can't walk without assistance – without perseverance.

But there are older men:
Nationalism, Classism, Racism, Sexism, Fascism.
They meet daily at the corner of Repetition and Fear.
They pound the pavement for pundits.
They scream about injustice while stepping on heads.

Mr. Check and Mr. Balance (still both white),
cower in the corner.
They've been to this rodeo before.
They now wear clown make-up, and dance with the big bulls from
each party until they've lost their breath.

Who's missing? Power? Ideology?
Those belong to the ruling class, the money class.
The class that pedals in illusion and times gone by.

The monitor is beeping. We are approaching flatline.
Hold on, old man. Hold on!
We'll stop talking and start doing. I promise…I think.
We'll rise up! We'll fight back!

Let me just adjust my recliner and turn the channel.
Sorry, old man. Maybe another time.

**MORTAR**

Is it a foreshock or aftershock?
There have been so many.
The only certainty –
It will knock this house down!

This fragile, decaying house.
Built with blocks of pain and anger, hunger and sickness,
With doctrine and despair, hate and jealousy.

The walls touch. The blocks intermingle,
but the mortar is disintegrating -
          Empathy, Compassion, Civility, Grace, Service.

The vibration runs under the walls,
softening and weakening the footholds.
The ripples grow to waves of frustration,
beating into the corner we've carved for ourselves.

The epicenter is hard to pinpoint, but irrelevant now.
The chasm it created is too deep,
the divide, too wide.

We resign ourselves to let it go.
We convince ourselves we can't stop it.
Resignation is easier than accountability.

So, we do nothing, as always,
nothing.
We let the rafters fall, and the windows shatter.
We don't look out or within, so it doesn't matter.

Soon, the earth will spin a thousand times,
and dance around the sun a thousand more,
in the void of space, where no one hears the screams.

The house will be swallowed,
the old will cave to ruin,
and new growth will begin.

Maybe.
It's hard to say how many chances we have.
New blocks will be set with mortar,
But who will the builders be?

## SHADOW SUN

It's not a springtime, happy sun anymore. There is a foreboding.
The shadows cast are somehow bigger than the whole expanse of
light.
There might occasionally be a calm breeze,
or a feeling of warmth.
Sometimes you can still rejoice after a long night,
when the darkness lifts, and the new day holds such promise.

But it's hard to fully open your eyes amidst the burning glare of reality.
To see, is to really see.
To observe is to recognize.

To watch the children playing in the park,
        without seeing the homeless man on the corner.
To notice the up arrows next to the stock market symbols,
        without flinching at the negative sign in your bank balance.
To be a dutiful consumer,
        without feeling the arrogance of the powerful, and the
desolation of the forgotten.

The view is tainted. The vision, distorted.
It's a winter sun now,
a white, acid-washed version of what was there before.

## INCESSANT

Dissonance: a disharmonious clash.
The crunchy chord that makes the hair on the back of your neck stand
on end.
Usually subtle and fleeting.

Then, the synchronous vibration of Resonance.
Full and reverberating.
The singularity of the theta wave.
Sweet relief.

We're stuck in between, crunching it out,
banging the tuning fork on our head, over and over.
Hearing nothing. Recognizing nothing.
Experiencing nothing. Forgiving nothing.

Begging just for silence. The resolution. The break.
The reset, so the ebb and flow can continue.
But for now, we wait,
Doomed to replay the same song ad infinitum.

**COMPLICIT  (The Fading Orange Glow)**

When you live your life without purpose or vision,
And the thing you love most is spite and derision,

When all that you have goes to ones who have all,
And no charity is left for the weak and small.

When you look at the world through your own narrow lens,
And you seek to do harm, with your words or your hands,

Then, you aren't a Christian, a Patriot, or Saint.
Those things you can't be when you lack all restraint.

I'm guessing they all require self-less devotion,
Hard, when you're set on your own self-promotion.

So, stop spreading fear with labels, it's gross.
We can't claim to help "these," while we persecute "those."

Stop grandstanding, soapboxing, and pretending you're smart.
It still doesn't change the depth of your heart.

Stop quoting scripture and constitutional law,
You obviously don't understand what you saw.

Stop waving your flags, stop thumping your bible,
If you intend to divide, then you are still libel!

You started from privilege, your tank is half-full,
Yet, you still exude hate, when push comes to pull.

Pray to be sweeter, then hide 'til you're healed.
We'll keep things running, while your hate is repealed.

Own your behavior, it's simply a must,
'Cuz you can't scream for justice, while being unjust.

It's time to put "we" ahead of the "me,"
Stop claiming that sacrifice means you're not free.

For those drowning in vitriol, and mired in hate,
You can pivot, and fix it, it isn't too late.

Help others now, without compensation,
Do it with kindness, and without hesitation.

All people have value, I hope you find yours,
Before your insanity leads to more wars.

We must all face our demons, that much is explicit,
Or we can't point the finger, we'll all be complicit.

**SPACKLE IS KING**

It's time for the patch job again.
Holes are everywhere.

Some are large enough to sound the alarm,
Funding, teacher shortages, vouchers.
Shootings, over-testing, pandemics.
Most aren't big enough to see the green grass on the other side.
Others are pinpricks that seem insignificant to outsiders,
but left to fester, threaten structural integrity.
Devaluing, blaming, proselytizing.
Strategizing, coping, excusing.

The details are nefarious,
Whispered in hallways,
Cried over at lunches,
Cussed out on drives home.
Bargains made in the dead of night.
"Two more years and I'm free."
"Fifteen years is too many."
"God, just get me to next week."

This structure has been damaged for a while.
There are no supports left,
It's held up by sheer determination,
Hard work covering the broken promises.
The bodies in overcrowded classrooms bolster it on one side.
Political aspirations and uninformed opinions push back from the
other.
It's still upright, but man, it's wobbly.
Literally crumbling before our eyes.

We balance it on the backs of our children,
We leverage it on a sick and dying work force.

Nothing in the current system can anchor the wall.
Not data collection, graphs, or rubrics,
Not submitting lesson plans a year in advance,
Not S.T.E.M.-ing away fine arts or recess,
Not pedagogy, fidelity, or rigor,
Not regurgitating a catalog of evaluation benchmarks,
Not a growth mindset, or trauma-informed practices,
Not administrative guidance, a.k.a threatening and coercing,

It's time to trowel on some more mud. Spread it around.
A nice thick coat will surely save the wall. Paint it. Dress it up.
Make it look pretty with "Ah-ha moments" and taxonomy,
With Common Core and learning analytics.
It looks so cute with a mission statement hung by the office,
Signed by all the stakeholders and covered in rainbow handprints.
But it's still the same crappy structure,
held together with toothpicks, caffeine, and desperation.

Slap on some incentives for the experts working in middle
management.
Allow them to dress comfortably (for a small fee),
give them free pastries once a year,
A whole 20 minutes for lunch,
Supply them with "Burnout Management Techniques."
In the end, the jargon doesn't matter,
The incentives don't matter.
If you can't fix it, just cover it up.

Add texture, or smooth it out. It hardly matters.
You can work miracles with spackle.

Spackle is king.
Spackle fixes everything.

## TIDE RELENTLESS

The bathtub is full.
One more toe in,
one more swish,
and the dam breaks.

Waterfall to tsunami,
tsunami to flood,
flood to decay,
decay to ruin.

There will be no coming back,
not for a long time,
not within our shared memory,
of what it was like to be in the Now.

The surfeit is all consuming,
even yet, before the porcelain cracks and crumbles.
Drip, drip, drip.
Spillage into every corner, every country, every pore.

Those on the edge, never able to get dry,
gasping for a gulp of air before the next wave.
Air no longer feels like air,
just an inhalation of dense denial.

The rot is extensive,
the mold, thick and toxic.
We pray for evaporation.
We pray for absolution, before saturation.

# OUT OF TIME

## RIGHT ON OUR FRONT PORCH

The porch looked unattended, broken, and clawed.
The style hinted that yesterday was important,
but the paint said, "as if."
I couldn't even look at the torn and faded patriotic bunting.
It seemed gruesome, knowing where it had led us.

I still feel the rage at the sea of red hats marching down the street,
their manhoods bolstered on their hips
or slung across their shoulders.
Screaming at us to get in our houses,
their hate pouring from their pores and prompting the pyre that
swallowed us up.

We deserved it - all of it.

We couldn't be bothered.
We tuned out the daily politics,
because it was too hard, "too much."
We just wanted to watch a good parade,
and pump up our averageness as greatness.

We were ready,
sitting on the porch with popcorn and lemonade,
the culpable victims of laziness, selfishness, greed,
befuddlement, indifference, and tardy outrage.
Entertainment quickly turned to shock and terror.

The signs were there,
long before the rhetoric.
Long before the flawed system reared its ugly head,
the undercurrent of unrest,
poked at the underskirts of suburban illusion.

It was not great for everyone, to be sure,
only for those who had a voice.
They tried to tell us.
They screamed at us to listen.
But they were drowned out by the marching band and the firetruck
sirens.

The porch still stands.
An ugly reminder of regret.
I would like to think it's in defiance,
but it's not a monument to resistance.
It's an effigy to compliance.

I don't care that it used to be my porch.
I want to knock it down,
sledgehammer its memories.
I have no right to them anymore.
I let it happen, and so did we all.

We have to own it,
along with every other part of our horrible history.
Sometimes all we can do is hold hands and cry.
We can stare at the porch and wonder why,
Or we can build a new house.

# INDEPENDENCE DAY

To        bar -    b-       que      or      screeeeeeeeeeeeeeeam.
It        feels    like     a        bad     dreeeeeeeeeeeeeeeeam.
Fire      works    and      a        good    beeeeeeeeeeeeeeeeeeer,
Can-      not      squelch  all      the     feeeeeeeeeeeeeeeeeear.
It's      hard/to  eat      brats    and     chiiiiiiiiiiiiiiiiiiiiiiiiiips,
In/our    self-    made     apoc-    a-      lyyyyyyyyyyyyyyyyyypse.
We/try    to/keep  our      fear     at      baaaaaaaaaaaaaaaaaay,
But/we    doom     scroll   all      damn    daaaaaaaaaaaaaaaaaaay.
It's/also/hard/on/one's/careeeeeeeeeeeeeeeeeeeeeeeeeeeeeeeer,
When/the/outlook/is/seveeeeeeeeeeeeeeeeeeeeeeeeeeeeeeeeeeere.
Watch/the/news/and/cry/at/niiiiiiiiiiiiiiiiiiiiiiiiiiiiiiiiiiiiiiiiiiiiight,
'Cuz/we/know/things/just/aren't/riiiiiiiiiiiiiiiiiiiiiiiiiiiiiiiiiiiiiiiiiiiiight.
Then/go/to/work/and/answer/phooooooooooooooooooooooooones,
Try/not/to/obsess/on/the/unknoooooooooooooooooooooooowns.
Then/once/a/year/on/seven/fooooooooooooooooooooooooooour,
We/just/party/and/ignoooooooooooooooooooooooooooooooore.
Blow/shit/up/and/wine/and/diiiiiiiiiiiiiiiiiiiiiiiiiiiiiiiiiiiiiiiiiine,
And/pretend/everything's/fiiiiiiiiiiiiiiiiiiiiiiiiiiiiiiiiiiiiiiiiiiiine.

## THE STICKING PLACE

We reached the unnatural balance,
the only place we could go when the coven's offering plates were
overflowing. It's the place where heads roll.
The place where the bankers trip over each other to gather the last
kitchen scraps.
Eventually, even if he refuses to take off his gold shoes,
Jack can't be nimble or quick.
The people now hold the candle stick.
They've weighed their options and no amount of elbow grease can
balance the scales.

The stage was set. The people clocked out and waited.
The uppercrusties countered with slick maneuvers, but they couldn't
shove enough of their friends out of the way to get to their dark
corners.
Their essence spilled out on the scale -
reputation, 401ks, bonds and stock options,
bonuses paid for through attrition, bribery, lobbying, and debauchery.
They started to fidget as the layers of their persona were stripped
away and the scale began to self-correct.

The crowd saw the nakedness before them.
Once again, the cast-offs were burdened with empathy.
They knew what it was to be weighed down.
They offered a deal:
"One of you, just one of you has to take responsibility.
Tell us you're sorry. Tell us you mean it.

Cry, beg for mercy and show us you now understand what it means,
          to have a knee on your neck,
                    a foot to your ribs,
                         a padlock on your mouth.
Prove to us that you understand what you did and why it was wrong,
and we will give you back your cloaks.

We will un-stick you from this place."

Silence.

Loud silence.
Deafening silence.

A few feigned a step forward,
but were held back.
Blue bloods don't break ranks.
Suddenly, one burst free from the grip and stepped off the scale. "I'm
sor..."

Murmurs floated.

"Shush, listen to him. He wants to confess."
"Good for you. Be brave. You can do it!"
"You don't even need to speak, brother.
Just pay your corporate taxes and you can keep your kingdoms."

Suddenly, he panicked "Wait, that wasn't part of the deal. You said..."

"We said PROVE to us.
The pay is your proof."
He turned and reached for the scale, but his species denied him.
He jumped for the Fulcrum. The mechanism broke.

The hive of 'entrepreneurs' hit the ground.
Funny thing, capitalists don't bounce.
The pile of corporate corpses was just high enough for the bottom-
barrelers to have something to grab on to.
They let go of their bootstraps and hoisted themselves on the
wreckage.
Most didn't spit on or disparage the new fodder under their feet.
But they also didn't stop for the desperation that grabbed at their
ankles.

Finally, they could see the horizon, instead of the pit.
The sun only rises for the huddled masses when it sets for the silver spoons.
"What so proudly we hailed, in the twilight's last gleaming."

## GAME OF BLAME

Wrecked again—in disbelief,
Disillusion and denial,
Thinking things were different now,
But turns out all the while,

We were playing different games,
Mine had higher stakes,
You weren't playing by the rules,
Some say, that's just the breaks.

Excuses try to weave your web,
And put me in a trance.
You'd think, since playing so many times,
I'd sometimes win by chance.

I guess when patterns re-emerge,
They're easy to restore,
It doesn't take a super sleuth,
I knew them from before.

So now decisions must be made,
To confront and magnify,
Or sweep it back under the rug,
Ignore, discount, deny.

# THE LOWDOWN

Talk to me like I'm stupid,
Make me understand,
How we can make claims on water,
Or why we monopolize land.

If we have to have wealth to prosper,
Or own power to hold back the night,
Then the basic needs of our species,
Are no longer a human right.

And if human rights are bartered,
And sold to the richest few,
Then why do we need the buyers?
We just need to change our view.

They can't own it all if we don't accept it,
They can shout and try to condemn,
But when the sun comes up in the morning,
There's still more of us than them.

## ASSHOLES ANONYMOUS

Hi, my name is Greed. And I'm and addict.

*"Hi, Greed."*

It's been about 47 seconds since I last indulged.
I've been trying to work the steps.
I'll admit, I am powerless over my own influence.

Moving on to step 3, I've decided to turn myself over to God.
Our relationship is great.
His minions have talked about me in the pulpit for years.
I think some of the preachers even read my book,
because they're really good at focusing on what's important,
like the collection plate, tithing, the bottom line,
investments… "missions."

I've been working on a list of people I have wronged, so I can make amends.
Yikes! It's a long one. (*Greed chuckles*)
I might have to just skip that step.
I know it's frowned upon, but I'm sure some of you have done it.

I see a few familiar faces in the room tonight, you can back me up.
What's up, Gluttony?

*(Gluttony tips his hat.)*

How's it hanging Envy? Heh, heh. We've worked together on a few projects. Good to see you again. Oh, and look, one of my favorites, Pride.

*(Pride and Envy high five. Greed continues to scan the room.)*

Of course, I can't forget about Lust. Hey gorgeous, looking good…REAL good.

*(Lust blows a kiss.)*

Sloth, you're just keeping it real. Workin' hard, or hardly working. Am I right? Am I right?
And Wrath, I can't believe you are even still hanging with us.
You're making a BIG comeback.
You might even surpass me.

*(Greed chortles.)*   What am I saying? Who can beat me?

*(Crowd cheers, except for Pride. He and Wrath storm out together.
Lust suggests an orgy. Envy's pissed he didn't think of it first.
Sloth and Gluttony decide to order pizza and take a nap instead.)
(Greed, Lust, and Envy join hands to end the meeting.
Pride and Wrath yell through the open window.)*

"God, grant me the Audacity to change whatever the fuck I want. The Conviction to make it as horrible as possible for everyone involved. And the Influence to make sure laws are passed to protect us."

*(Greed grabs his tumbler of whisky on the way out the door.)*

Great meeting everyone. I'm ringing the bell at the NYSE tomorrow.
Then I'll see you after, at the Capitol.

# CHRONIC

Too late for a re-do.
Now, it's the coping,
The managed care,
The attitude adjustment.

There are chores with illness.
Filling pill caddies,
Tests and appointments,
Paperwork and phone calls.

Logging new symptoms,
Researching new treatments,
Finding new doctors who'll listen--
Who won't blame it all on P.M.S.

The what-ifs, the if-onlys, and the remember-whens,
Knock nightly on your brain,
Don't answer, they're vicious.
They thrive on second guessing, and sowing doubt.

Disease adds up.
It's a thief and a beggar.
Robbing you of normalcy,
And always asking you for a payday.

It's also an accountant,
Keeping tabs on the bad days,
Always bartering for more.
Always selling healthy organs to the highest bidder.

But the biggest bitch, is pain.
She's evil, and she makes no bargains.
She holds all the cards,
And she knows it.

She might give you a respite to catch your breath,
But only so she can re-group.
She'd make deals with the devil,
But even the devil doesn't like her.

## OF BROKEN THINGS

Bill of sale:
- One Black man sentenced to life for trying to steal a pair of hedge clippers
- One white man charged with rape, serving one-month probation
- One Senator getting rich on stock tips while voting for de-regulation
- One Vigilante on a partisan press tour
- One twice-impeached con man still pretending to be a statesman
- One Representative cleaning their gun during a Veteran's Affairs hearing
- One trans person beaten by a mob
- One diabetic dead from not being able to afford medication
- One white police officer still employed after killing a shy black teen
- One couple bankrupt from family illness
- One billionaire claiming to be altruistic while paying no tax
- One entertainment network posing as a news organization
- One gay teen committing suicide after conversion therapy
- One child disillusioned by school from constant testing
- One child murdered by abusive parents
- One child killed in school shooting
- One child snatched from parents at border

Methods of Payment:
(Check all that apply)
__outdated constitution   __biased judicial system      __confused populace
__desperate education system   __broken tax code      __corrupted legislature
__prison industrial complex      __unscrupulous insurance system
__grossly capitalist society

Payment due on demand. Failure to submit new form of payment will result in continuing purchase of products listed above, causing total bill to reach unsustainable limits.
Taxes and shipping not included.

No guarantees.
No warranties.
No refunds or exchanges.

# MENDING TIME

## THE WEAVER

The weaver builds. The weaver destroys.
Over, under, pull through,
Each strand a truth or a lie. Each strand strengthens the garment.

The weave is more impenetrable with each pass.
Solid, in its fairness or folly.
Sturdy, in its rightness or wrongness.

Examine the threads. Look at their meaning.
Don't throw on the cape just because it's finished and pretty.
Pull it apart. Stomp on it. Scream at it to reveal its nature.

Truth is sewn back together easily. The pieces fit – make sense.
The pattern can be repeated and healed together with time and
analysis.

Lies fall apart.
Damaged goods expose themselves under the harsh lamp of reality.
Threads disintegrate. Facts weave.

Beware the weaver, but trust time.
With patience, the ultimate artificer reveals his craft.
Threads disintegrate. Facts weave.

## THE SAVING DANCE

Ninety-seven saves, according to the abacus.
Maybe more like four thousand.

That's what we do. You and I – we save each other.

We can count it in peacock feathers, or the times I
soaked your shirt with my insanity and tears.

We can measure it by the moon's cycle,
your turn to shine, mine is to shadow.
My turn to wax or wane in joy,
while you pay bills and take care of life.

San Marco's tiles can't predict the real number.
Big Ben can't predict the frequency.
Weekly and weakly I rise, you fall,
You flourish, I flounder.
That's how we do.

You cause the wound, I lick it.
I crackle apart, you glue.
I stab, you stitch.

That is our love dance.
Not 2.2 children, or a nice lawn
or vacations, or photos with smiles,
or even paid bills and a device to stream.

The dance is in the saving.

## WHEN BREATHERS ARE BENT

I feel the trees.
Their age and sturdiness always seeking to comfort.
Touching the bark almost stings.
I know their pain.

Not because they talk, but because they beg us to listen.
Needles fall. Leaves crumple. Fruit dries. Acorns crack.

We want to believe it's all natural,
A lifecycle of sacrifice,
for our cutting and chopping and burning and usurping.
But apathy is destructive.

How else shall we satiate our appetite?
How else to quell our need to self-sabotage?

We know this - the trees will stay.
They will stay to the bitter end.
They will breathe with us. They will breathe for us.
What shall we do to be worthy of trees?

I sing them a silent lullaby to make amends.
The bough bends.

**A GLIMPSE OF SKY**

The cleaning has begun,
but before the renewal, comes chaos.
I scrape the filth to release the under layers,
The sediment is stubborn.
The footholds--robust.

Many are mired in the dregs.
It's almost comfortable to sink to the bottom.
There's lots of company there,
good company with stories of reminiscence and familiarity.
Looking back is fun. Staying there, is dangerous.

From the surface, it's easy to overlook a hole in the ground,
even one filled with screams of want.
But from the bottom of the well, the only view is the hole above,
the glimpse of sky,
the promise of expanse,
the illusion of excess.

So we climb,
sometimes on each other.

We find the cracks to wedge our feet and hands,
Occasionally we gain some ground, but there's not much traction in
desperation.
The walls get slippery when you're covered in muck;
the carefully crafted muck,
made of droppings tossed carelessly down the well by the light
stealers.

They yell down and grin.
"Don't give up," they say,
As they wink and fist bump each other with greasy palms,

They bid their caddies to toss another coin down the well,
Knowing the fight for the few coins, will be to the death.

They move on to play another eighteen,
Unaware, or unmoved,
by the tussle below.
Meanwhile, the rasping and grinding has begun.
The erosion is faster now, because more are digging.

People form teams, unions, class actions--voting leagues.
Activists charge their batteries on the hubbub.
Though the sides are still slick, the determination is palpable.
Serious tools are disseminated and shared,
No more spoons to dig our owns graves.

Gardeners furrow with their spades,
Plumbers gouge with their pipes,
Nurses carve with their scalpels,
Teachers scrape with their rulers,
Cooks scoop with spatulas.

Exhaustion sets in.
The determination is there, but the progress is slow,
especially when more, who were once comfortable,
fall through the cracks, and into the hole.
Kicked in by inflation, interest rates, and stifling debt.

So we pause. We dig deep--inside.
We gather the abuse, the ridicule, and the insults-
"Burger flipper," "babysitter," "pencil pusher," "snowflake,"
We use the rage to wad them up and jab them into the wall built
around us.
Not the wall to keep others out, but the wall made to fence us in.

The well is drying from the bottom and closing from the top,
while the bedrock continues to crumble.
It's scary now, but this is the long game.

It's make-it or break it time.

This is what we came for.

Forget the hatchets and pickaxes,
Lock arms!
Two are better than one, four are better than two.
Form the rungs, reach out for the hungry,
Grab the weak and sick, and pass them up.
They've been here the longest.

The human chain, that's our salvation,
Our only way out of the well.

## GEOPOLITICAL BUBBLESTUFF

I dip in the goo and swirl through the magic.
Denial is sparkly, and pretty, and tragic.

Waving the wand, I decide what appears,
Caution and experience, or prejudice and fears.

I know the bubbles created before,
Through borders, religion, resources, and war.

Through military propaganda, and human rights violations,
Through shady trade deals and disarming small nations.

Through nationalism, racism, and all things divisive,
The tools of our leaders are rarely incisive.

We can't change it all, even if we plan it.
The bubbles we've made, still cover the planet.

So, we start with our home, our neighborhood, our town,
When others make bubbles, we blow them all down.

We vote for the people with a plan, and with soul,
That's how we start to make the world whole.

We fire the zealots, and un-employ takers,
We interview those who want to be new map makers.

We tear down the walls, and stop being fine,
With blaming those born just over the line.

**THE UNWIND**

I washed off the make-up of the first half of my life.
I stopped wearing earrings and bangles.
I stopped using hairspray to make sure my hair stays fixed and perfect.
I pee when I want. I eat, sleep, and read when I want.

I mean to call, but mostly I don't.
I mean to write, but who are we kidding?

I mostly watch the leaves fall and the clouds roll on.

And I don't cry – at least like I used to.
My face doesn't get hot and feel like exploding.
My lungs breathe and my heart beats,
without me reminding it why it needs to.

It's slower now, and it's okay.

# IGNORING TIME

## INSTRUCTIONS

Where shall you set sail, my child?
>Where the water is shallow, and the current is light. I shall ride the waves and be brave in the rapids, just like you taught me.

Where shall you touch down, my child?
>Where the ground is stiff and sturdy. I shall make a dwelling that stands strong against the blast, just like you taught me.

Where shall you plant, my child?
>Where the soil is rich, and the sun warm. I shall sow the seedlings and prune the vines, so I am always prepared to harvest, just like you taught me.

Where shall you rest, my child?
>Where the prairie grass bends soft. I shall cushion my head on the plumes and dream of my future, just like you taught me.

When you fail, how shall you prepare to travel, and root, and grow, and restore, my child?
>I shall prosper, just like you taught me.

I can't teach you to prosper, my child. I sailed the rough seas. I landed in the sinking sands. I reaped unviable harvests, and I laid in nightmares awake.

>Then why did you sing me stories of success?
>Why did you tell me the arrow always lands on the target?

I didn't teach you to ride the waves, I taught you to be brave.
I didn't teach you to find solid ground, I taught you to stand strong.
I didn't teach you to sow and prune, I taught you to be prepared.
I didn't teach you to rest, I taught you to dream.

I didn't teach you to loose the arrow, I taught you to be the arrow!

# THE QUILT

Sewing, sewing here I go,
Making patterns to and fro,
Needles trace the path I leave,
Forming pictures as I weave,

Ego captured in a square,
Exposed and taut, just lying there,
Waiting for a trace of guilt,
to cover it and make this quilt.

Instead I cut this ego out,
I stare at it, thrash it about.
I berate it for the pain it's caused,
But it wasn't what I thought it was.

Addicted to repeated tropes,
Seen only under microscope.
It's not a devil, just benign,
The stitching is the only sign.

Threads of insult, woven tight,
Seam-rip that out, to make things right.
It's not from pride, but lack, we crow,
And seeing that is how we grow.

My student, Ego, daily learns,
to ditch old painful loops and turns.
Reaction ruts won't be allowed,
Discernment is my needle now.

I stitch it in a prominent place,
Not to brag, but offer grace.
Cultivation cures the doubt,
For all that's sewn, can be ripped out.

## NORMALIZING IDLENESS

It's hard not to run when time seems short.
Running is the devil.
Exercise? Fine, yes, good.
But not running because you can't remember how to walk anymore.

No worries, remediations are available.
      Make a list,
            ask for help,
                  phone a friend,
And of course, the dreaded…meditate.

Come on, there's no time for breakfast, let alone yoga and a hot bath.
Keeping the pace is mandatory. Planning ahead is essential.
Falling apart - imminent.

Slowing seems impossible. Recovery is harder.

Sit, until the urge to conquer passes.
It could take between 4 minutes and 2 years.
Decompression is a marathon. Illness is a sprint.

Watch the sky. Keep watching after it starts to get boring.
Patterns emerge, followed by insights,
Followed by bliss.

Hold a hand, even if it's your own.
Squeeze until you feel the sour tug at the corner of your eye.
Embrace the catharsis.
Assign it no shame.

Inhale…Exhale,

Inhale,

Exhale.

## AGENDA DAY 1

Get up,
consult calendar,
make phone calls,
tackle to-do list,
clean,
take a 3-minute break,
order stuff,
buy stuff,
arrange stuff,
throw old stuff away to make room for new stuff,
question life choices,
reject judgement about internal debate about existential crisis,
own judgement about internal debate about existential crisis,
wash two dishes,
feel guilty for falling asleep while making new to-do list for tomorrow.


## AGENDA DAY 2

Get up,
change into daytime pajamas,
play with dog,
walk around,
eat something,
take a nap,
stretch,
read, sing, dance.

## AGENDA DAY 3

Get up

## I SHALL SING IT FOR YOU AGAIN

My voice was weak, tattered with age and use.
I tried to use it for justice,
but often the words came out sharp instead of pointed.
Pent up anger adds color to words in unintentional ways.

I tried to use it for inspiration,
but it sounded less like hope, and more like a textbook of good
intentions.
I tried to use it for resiliency,
But it's hard to convince others to move forward when you're
backpedaling up a hill.

I had to dig deeper to find the truth.
I'm not even sure I could have found it with a map.
I needed time.
Time to chronologically, and physically distance myself from trauma.

I needed space.
Room to navigate with less guidance, but more direction.
With less planning, but more of a plan.
With less certainty, but more conviction.

My voice wasn't useless. It was buried.
I had been using it wrong for way too long,
I forgot I could use it at all.
I forgot I wanted to.

Little by little, I picked up my pen.
I spoke with curiosity instead of certainty,
With humility, instead of condescension.
With questions instead of instructions.

And the funniest thing happened.
My tone evened out. My timbre improved.
My voice wasn't just a nail; it was how I the hammered it in.
It wasn't just a trumpet; it was how I played it.

So, I vocalize, and rehearse.
Only the best words are allowed now.
Craft is equal to intention.
Process is equal to purpose.

I lay them down with grace.
I offer them up in sacrifice.
I strive for creation over masterpiece,
For paint splattered on the canvas, rather than kept neatly in a jar.

I lift my voice in service to the universe.
I step out on to the ledge, with no hope of a net.
I shall breathe deeply. I shall endure.
And I shall sing for you again.

# A FIX-ED PURPOSE

To wear my duster in the rain,
To make my art, despite my pain,
To simply live, but not be plain,
That's where I shall begin.

To embrace this challenged millennium,
To be concerned, without the numb,
To write a poignant requiem,
And play it on my violin.

To build a treehouse with reclaimed logs,
To listen without monologues,
To have one hundred and seventy dogs,
And take some more vacations.

To keep my sight until I die,
To always learn and question why,
To forever enjoy the sky,
And all its constellations.

To scratch the itch that can't be scratched,
To trust a plan before it's hatched,
To heal a wound that can't be patched,
And always be of service.

To boldly look into the void,
To practice craft while still employed,
To see my children overjoyed,
That is my fix-ed purpose.

# EPILOGUE



The Hateful will peddle disdain,
Be the balm.

The Impoverished will struggle to persevere,
Defend with vigilance.

The Powerful will fight for complacency,
Cause a solid ruckus!